187 Men to Avoid

A Survivial Guide for the
Romantically Frustrated Woman

Dan Brown

Formerly Writing As

Danielle Brown

BERKLEY BOOKS, NEW YORK

THE BERKLEY PUBLISHING GROUP
Published by the Penguin Group
Penguin Group (USA) Inc.
375 Hudson Street, New York, New York 10014, USA
Penguin Group (Canada), 90 Eglinton Avenue East, Suite 700, Toronto, Ontario M4P 2Y3, Canada
(a division of Pearson Penguin Canada Inc.)
Penguin Books Ltd., 80 Strand, London WC2R 0RL, England
Penguin Group Ireland, 25 St. Stephen's Green, Dublin 2, Ireland (a division of Penguin Books Ltd.)
Penguin Group (Australia), 250 Camberwell Road, Camberwell, Victoria 3124, Australia
(a division of Pearson Australia Group Pty. Ltd.)
Penguin Books India Pvt. Ltd., 11 Community Centre, Panchsheel Park, New Delhi—110 017, India
Penguin Group (NZ), Cnr. Airborne and Rosedale Roads, Albany, Auckland 1310, New Zealand
(a division of Pearson New Zealand Ltd.)
Penguin Books (South Africa) (Pty.) Ltd., 24 Sturdee Avenue, Rosebank, Johannesburg 2196, South Africa

Penguin Books Ltd., Registered Offices: 80 Strand, London WC2R 0RL, England

187 MEN TO AVOID

Copyright © 1995 by Dan Brown.
Published by arrangement with the author.
Book design by Jill Dinneen.

PRINTING HISTORY
Berkley trade paperback edition / August 1995

ISBN: 0-425-21504-0

PRINTED IN THE UNITED STATES OF AMERICA

10   9   8   7   6   5

*"The trick of love is all
in the choosing."*

—Anonymous

*"As long as you know
that most men are children,
you know everything."*

—Coco Chanel

187 Men To Avoid...

Men who dress their dogs.

Men who eat

Kraft Macaroni & Cheese

more than once a week.

Men who wear

spandex biker shorts anywhere

other than on their bike.

Men who "do" lunch.

Men who have a

stuffed Garfield stuck anywhere.

Men with little, naked, metal women

on their mud flaps.

Men who trade baseball cards.

Men who cried when Cheers went off the air.

Men with electric nose hair trimmers.

Men who know where

Elvis

was last sighted.

Men who live with their mothers.

Men who get

their news from

The National Enquirer.

Men with dogs named "Scooter."

Men who use the

Home Shopping Network.

Men who have been

published in the Penthouse Forum.

Men who show their scars.

Men who think

"safe sex" means

locking the bedroom door.

Men who "Brake for BINGO."

Men who think farting is cute.

Men who play the tambourine.

Men with

license plate frames that read:

SO MANY WOMEN, SO LITTLE TIME.

Men who insist on ordering for you.

Men who are still mad they never got

that Eagle Scout badge.

Men who think Lamaze is

a famous French car race.

Men with belt buckles that say COORS.

Men who "honk if they're horny."

Men who moonwalk.

Men who consider Super Bowl Sunday

a religious holiday.

Men who wear full army fatigues

grocery shopping.

Men who say, "Have a good one."

Men with plastic houseplants.

Men with imitation-zebra car seat covers.

Men who pee in the shower.

Men who insist they'd be happy

to take a male *birth control pill*

if one existed.

Men who wake up at night

screaming, "How was I to know

she was only fifteen!"

Men who "pop wheelies."

Men who wear dickeys.

Men who think baking soda is a beverage.

Men who own a ThighMaster.

Men who insist they read

the Sports Illustrated *swimsuit issue*

for the sports journalism.

Men who play Nintendo.

Men who don't wear underwear.

Men who can sing

the entire Gilligan's Island theme

from memory.

Men who make balloon animals.

Men who stir-fry.

Men with centerfolds in their gym lockers.

Men who watch American Gladiators.

Men who play Twister.

Men with "issues."

Men who own the album

Zamphir, Master of the Pan Flute.

Men who truly believe pro-wrestling

should be an Olympic sport.

Men who have past lives.

Men who wish

they'd been born

a woman.

Men who drink

generic beer.

Men who say,

"Okey dokey."

Men who

"just want to be friends."

Men who bought

the Ginsu knife set.

Men who own more than

one model of the U.S.S. Enterprise.

Men whose homes have

that "litter box" smell.

Men with hairy moles.

Men who

consider burping on command

a marketable skill.

Men with

pierced anything.

Men with

fake Rolex watches.

Men with

real Rolex watches.

Men who say,

"Ciao."

Men with their

initials shaved into

their sideburns.

Men who eat Pop-Tarts.

Men who wear capes.

Men who consider

Cream of Wheat

a home-cooked meal.

Men who comb

their hair across the bald spot.

Men who say the last thing

they want to do is hurt you.

Men who

KEEP ON TRUCKIN'!

Men who own

Chia Pets.

Men who write

self-help books for women.

Men who pump up

their sneakers.

Men who tell

knock-knock jokes.

Men who pretend they know what

they're doing when they smell the cork.

Men who

call collect.

Men who

have phone sex.

Men who miss

The Village People.

Men who think

Fellini is a pasta dish.

Men who actually purchased

The Helsinki Formula.

Men with

Playboy Bunny car fresheners.

Men who eat

breakfast cereal for dinner.

Men who

wear medallions.

Men who consider

a tractor pull a cultural event.

Men who read

Dear Abby.

Men who think yeast infections

cause moldy bread.

Men who know more than

10 slang words for breasts.

Men with

fanny packs.

Men who

read their horoscope.

Men who prefer

scalp surgery over balding.

Men with

wind chimes.

Men who believe

the McDonald's McLean is health food.

Men who switched to

Pepsi Clear for health reasons.

Men who buy

Magnum condoms.

Men who

play the harp.

Men who carry satchels.

Men with

vanity plates like

BMW4DAN or OKGUY.

Men who use

self-tanning lotion.

Men who bring

their telephones to dinner.

Men who

use Binaca.

Men who

cut their own hair.

Men who think a

thesaurus is a dinosaur.

Men who keep a condom

in their wallet . . . just in case.

Men who watch

Oprah.

Men who

collect comic books.

Men who'd

"rather be"

anywhere.

Men who work at carnivals.

Men who watch

the pre-game show.

Men who

wear tank tops.

Men with

plastic lawn flamingos.

Men who can't say

the word "menstruation."

Men named

Spike.

Men who light matches

on their zippers.

Men who swallow goldfish.

Men who use

spritz, mousse,

and gel.

Men with

pet rocks.

Men with

manicures.

Men who think

estrogen

is a fuel additive.

Men with yo-yos.

Men with

car stereos worth more

than their car.

Men with poodles.

Men who don't consider

your aerobics class

a real workout.

Men who don't like Disneyland.

Men with

Crock-Pots.

Men who saw

Rocky IV.

Men who need

dental floss holders.

Men who still refer to bras as

"over-the-shoulder boulder-holders."

Men who sleep in their clothes.

Men who own

extra styling attachments

for their blow-dryers.

Men with neon

shoelaces.

Men whose cars have anything

"ON BOARD."

Men whose necks

are thicker than

their thighs.

Men with tinted contact lenses.

Men who are

too cool to dance.

Men who think a bassoon is

an endangered species.

Men who wear

mesh shirts.

Men who've read

Crying, Caring, Coping.

Men who

decoupage.

Men with

AmberVision sunglasses.

Men who still do

cannonballs.

Men who promise

they'll respect you in the morning.

Men who

burn fake logs.

Men with truck tires that are

taller than they are.

Men who play air guitar.

Men who don't

separate their white and

colored laundry.

Men who still own

Silly Putty.

Men who own dogs

that are smaller than cats.

Men who think pesto is

Spanish for mosquito.

Men who play charades

more than once a year.

Men who

chant.

Men who

flick boogers.

Men with their nicknames

embroidered on their jackets.

Men who wear

Obsession.

Men who knit.

Men with

surfing scenes airbrushed

onto their van.

Men who shave in the car

on their way to work.

Men who buy power tools

they have no idea how to use.

Men who

don't flush.

Men who think ovulation

is a chocolate breakfast drink.

Men who won't

eat quiche.

Men who swear they've never seen a

Victoria's Secret catalog.

Men who

"burn rubber."

Men who have their dog's photo

on their coffee mug.

Men with

pectoral implants.

Men in

thong bathing suits.

Men who

eat Fluffernutter sandwiches.

Men who were

Born to Boogie!

Men in clogs.

Men who struggle

to decide between Original Recipe

and Extra Crispy.

Men who own hamsters.

Men who wear

cowboy boots but have never seen

a cow in their life.

Men with

beanbag furniture.

Men in

tights.

Men who

giggle.

Men who wash their cars

more than once a week.

Men with

monogrammed anything.

Men who eat

anything on a stick.

Men who

don't own an iron.

Men in

platform shoes.

Men who

own reptiles.

Men who

wear clip-on ties.

Men who think

a spatula is that bone they

broke playing football.

Men who finger-wrestle.

Men who eat

breakfast cereals

that have

mini-marshmallows.

Men who

read women's books . . .

(like this one).

About the Author

Dan Brown, *no longer disguised by the Danielle Brown pseudonym, lives in New England.*